Infrastructure: Social Profit Biz Basics

*Everything I Needed In Business I
Learned in the Bathroom*

Infrastructure:
Social Profit Biz Basics

*Everything I Needed In Business I
Learned in the Bathroom*

Thyonne Gordon, Ph.D

First Printing: 2014

ISBN 978-1-889210-06-3 PAPERBACK
ISBN 978-1-889210-04-9 ELECTRONIC

A Writer Space Publishing
4859 W. Slauson Ave. #299
Los Angeles, CA 90056

www.awriterspace.com
www.beyondstory.com

This book is in honor of
Warriors of
VISION
Igniting thought to
Programs of Change

Dr. Pearl Grimes, Coalition for At Risk Youth
Holly Robinson-Peete, HollyRod Foundation
Carolyn White-Washington, Sisters4Sisters
Andrea Humphrey, Hope Community Development Center
Charyn Harris, Project MuszEd
Meissa Wyatt, Foundation for Second Chances
Zander Lurie & Leah Bernthal, CoachArt
Debrah Constance, A Place Called Home
Lydia Floyd, Hands for Hope
Kelli Hogan, City Scholars
Mark Whitlock, Pastor, Community Activist
Rev. Cecil L. Murray, Pastor & Community Activist

And Dedicated To My Lovely Daughter
Matthia B. Sales
With vision you will find your passion.

See It, Believe It & Be It

Contents

Introduction

As a graduate of not just one college but three highly esteemed graduate institutions, you'd think most of my learning would be from the halls and classrooms of one of them. Yes, there was a fair share of learning at each.

Howard University, a prestigious historically Black College, taught me the power of voice using strong ideas and thoughts. I received a strong background in presentation skills, writing and speaking at the School of Communications. I also gained a network of friends who would go on to be powerhouses in their industries and business ventures.

At Pepperdine University, I earned an MBA focused on Cultural and Organizational Development. Forging through classes in Statistics and Business Theory backed with case studies, gave me a sound background in business management. I embraced Six Sigma processes and found meaning and practical applications with Contingency, Chaos and Systems theories.

Infrastructure: Social Profit Biz Basics

Finally, my studies at Fielding Graduate University allowed exploration down a path where I could combine two loves – research and writing. The more I studied, the deeper I went down the rabbit hole of learning and life. At Fielding, I would confirm that the processes and tools from the MBA were not as black and white as I had categorized them. The hues would create a significant shift in how I viewed business management.

During my educational pursuits, I would continue to ponder my place and stance in the business world. While figuring this out and incorporating my theoretical learning with practical experience, I realized a valuable lesson in transformational integration. This lesson would become a constant tool in how I managed business efforts and relationships in the future.

It came after a visit with my *forever* pastor, Rev. Cecil L. Murray. I met Dr. Murray when arriving in Los Angeles, California and finding the church, First A.M.E. This church would be where I would learn from my greatest teachers. During one period while lamenting over my purpose and place in the world, I visited Rev. Murray. In his wise and inspirational way he listened. He has a way of listening and redirecting (without letting you know he redirected) such that you feel like he actually answered you directly. On this occasion he answered by sending me to the then COO of the FAME Renaissance Community Development Program, Mr. Steve Johnson.

Steve seemed to have the same listening demeanor as Pastor Murray. I explained that I was starting a new position in the 501c3 arena and had no idea what to do. Furthermore, I didn't know if I should really even be at this company or in the space. After listening intently for about 20 minutes, Steve politely nodded his head in an understanding way, stood up and began leading me to the door of his office. I was very excited because I thought he was going to show me firsthand how to run the new business venture. I thought he was about to give me a walk around tour. I could sense we were about to have a "Yoda" moment, when Steve opened the office door and leaned into me saying, "Start in the bathrooms." He then gave me a warm shoulder embrace followed by a pat on the back and sent me on my way.

I stood outside his now closed office door confused, shaken and frustrated. What did he mean, "Start in the bathrooms?" What kind of wacky advice was that? I was perplexed and frustrated and ran to the nearest bathroom to yell, scream and have a quick boo hoo at being so lost. Looking in the mirror I felt like I'd wasted an entire morning and had no additional advice on what to do. I left that bathroom feeling rejected and lost.

When I arrived at work for my first day, I felt no more ready for the assignment than when I went for advice from my "guru's" of wisdom. After a walk thru of the facility, I was lead to my modest office to start work. I had no idea what to do, but the words from Steve continued to ring in my head, "Start in the bathrooms."

When I asked for the head of maintenance to come into my office and share with me what his duties were, everyone was taken aback. Not too many new COO's began their learning with the janitorial staff.

The main person, Raphael, shared about his work day and challenges for about 30 minutes until I interrupted asking, "What about the bathrooms?" He looked puzzled but began to tell me which bathrooms to use and which ones I should steer clear of. I asked him to take me to each bathroom—especially those he thought I shouldn't use. As we toured the bathrooms we began discussing how to make each better than the next. At the end of our walk thru I asked Raphael to write up a plan on what he would do to remedy the bathroom problems and the time frame it would take. On that day I committed to Raphael a statement that would throw him and the rest of the team off, for the next couple of months, "The bathrooms are my number one priority," I said and returned to my office.

The short end of this long story is a wonderful journey of transformation, building and growth. This struggling organization transformed from having two weeks of payroll into a trusted and secure multi-million dollar safe haven for youth. And, all of this began in the bathroom.

When starting in the bathroom, I never thought the lessons would come so quickly but each step of the process in the bathrooms, lead me to new revelations and in no time I realized everything I needed in business I was learning in the bathroom! Of course I appreciate my classroom knowledge but some of my best business practices were found in the bowels of the bathroom. Well, flush me away (pun intended)!

Now, I've decided to share the lessons I learned in an easy to read format. In this book, you will learn some business basics without having to go through years of professorship, classes and theories -- and for a lot less money than an MBA and Doctorate.

Now, this is in no way a statement that university learning is not valuable. As you can see from my introductory text, I thoroughly enjoyed my education and would not change a thing about my schooling (well other than the price). But use this book a "Cliffs Notes" into the world most call "nonprofit business basics."

Using the simple lessons in Everything I Needed In Business I Learned In the Bathroom, will help you manage teams more effectively, run your business more efficiently and grow your business into the prosperous space you desire.

The book is divided into three parts using concepts and ideas straight from the bowels of the bathroom. In each chapter we will start with the learning from the bathroom and how it relates to business. At the end of each section, you will get a Bathroom Biz Basics Tool to take away for your learning.

In this introductory book, you will learn about Infrastructure and the makings of your 501c3 endeavor. It's an easy read, which, quite frankly, you can finish behind a closed door, on a familiar seat. Yes! This is great bathroom reading material. Enjoy!

501c3:
The Business of Heart, Head & Soul

In this world where business is measured by a Wall Street status or how much companies make and take, I believe a shift must occur. This shift is based on the heart of a business. I know, many might note business as an entity does not have a heart. I say that business is a creative energy of people and it does.

With every client that's served, dollar that's earned and vendor that's affiliated, a steady beat occurs that gives the business a conscious how and why existence. And the beats are measured such that when there is a misstep, it causes a skip in that beat – and accordingly damage to that heart and ultimately to the business overall.

Starbuck's became one of fastest growing companies in the '90s because of the pulse that Howard Schultz helped shepherd. When he left and the company's beat began to go off, it was evident that the heart of the company was no longer the same. Upon his return he began to monitor and steadily socially conscious heartbeat of the company returned too.

That heartbeat is in every company and becomes evident as culture. Starbuck's culture happened to be a distinct care of the product and the customer as important. It was the type of beat that caused employees to care about not just the company, but the customers the company served. In his book, Onward: How Starbucks fought for Its Life Without Losing Its Soul," Schultz shares the story of an employee who gives a kidney to a regular customer. Yes, that sounds above and beyond the call of duty for any employee, but it wasn't just because that employee was a good person (and yes, they were great) but it was because of the culture that Starbucks created around care – care for each cup of coffee and care for each customer.

When we begin to focus on what value there is in giving goods and services as well as what we receive in return, we can grasp what a company's heart beat feels like. The idea is not so far-fetched. The giving begins with offering quality products and services for reasonable and fair pricing. However, it extends to being in sync with the communities in which our businesses reside as well as understanding and valuing the needs of the consumers.

There is enough to go around--if we are not so greedy as to hoard the extras.

In this equation of socially conscious businesses, the industry that society has labeled as "not for profit or nonprofit" organizations, have the opportunity to lead the way. These organizations understand the cause and affect of giving and the strong and steady heartbeat began at the inception of the idea to formulate a 501c3. These are the organizations that prioritize giving as a means of operating. Yet, as much as the giving aspect is understood, receiving and considering the core of such a business is often misinterpreted. A key element is evident in the label that begins with lack. And that lack projects a weakened heartbeat leading towards a needy trajectory verses a confident life changing one.

The 501c3 space is the only industry that is described by what is "not" done verses what "is" done. In this inaccurate affront to an industry providing on-purpose services and products, the public tends to view such organizations as poor and needy (just as much in need as the constituents served). With this impoverished mentality it is no wonder the difficulty nonprofits have in acquiring funds for mainly excellent services provided for society to work more holistically. In general 501c3's are viewed as beggars. Yet, in truth, every business "asks" for something and the true test in consumerism is whether or not the company delivers when the "ask" is met.

In my work in this space, I encourage organizations providing on-purpose services to stand up for their work with a strong heartbeat, which starts with embracing titles that better inform the work. Changing the labels that others have put on 501c3's is the first start to not only building stronger infrastructure, but also in empowering the entire community affiliate – employees, constituents and donors.

In the Everything I Needed In Business I Learned In The Bathroom book series, these organizations have been re-labeled as Social Profit Organizations. This is my own personal way of correcting the skip in the beat of the heart in the service community. This is the beginning of the shift I encourage.

Join me in uplifting the powerful work of Social Profit Organizations as positive and inspiring, by choosing our words carefully and specifically focused towards making a difference.

Enjoy the series and I look forward to hearing your feedback.

Chapter One:
Know Your Business

Bathroom: Where's Your Bathroom & What Type Is It?

Business: Know where you are & what you do.

In real estate, the top 3 important things about property are location, location and location. Just in case you didn't get the point, location is pretty important when buying a house. The locations of the rooms that are inside of a house are just as important. In particular, the location of the bathroom can be critical.

If you are wondering why it's important, think about a visitor coming to your home and needing to use the bathroom. Let's say this visitor had to go through two bedrooms, a kitchen and a sitting room just to get to the toilet. Would you really want them going through your house in that manner? Probably not! That's why a properly situated restroom is important. Knowing where that restroom is and how it's situated is important too.

Now how does this apply to business? In case you're thinking it has to do with your building or where you're located you're on the wrong track. It's a little more focused than that. Location in terms of your social profit has to do with where you are in your business?

Are you a beginning business with limited resources? Are you mid-sized and not sure how to expand further? Or, have you reached a maximum capacity where you are trying to figure out how to leverage into a franchise or other equity building area? These questions are essential in understanding how to run your business. When we know where we are, it's easier to get where we want to go.

Answer the following questions to understand where you are in your business:

1. Do you have a written document that explains your business?
2. Do you have a budget or income and expense statement that tells how much money is coming in and how much money is going out?
3. Do you have a team of people to help support your business?

Infrastructure: Social Profit Biz Basics

If you answered yes to all three of these questions then you have actually established the basics of a good business structure with a foundation. If your answer is no to any of these questions, then your foundation is weak and needs some work.

Now you may ask, how does this business issue relate to a bathroom experience? Well, think about it. Knowing where you are and what you are supposed to do in any situation helps you get the job done. Especially in the bathroom!

In the bathroom, there are certain things that take place. You can use the toilet, take a shower, shave, primp in the mirror, or just isolate yourself from the world. The point is, when you know what you're supposed to do in any one place, you can get the job done.

We all know where to go in the restroom to get whatever job done that we need to get done. We also know what to do while we're in the restroom. The business world is no different. We should know where we are and where we are headed as well as why we're headed there.

Where you are in business is easily explained with the bathroom examples listed below.

Check out how each bathroom type serves a purpose in the Tool Kit of lessons below.

What Do You Do?
Quarter Bath – Mission / Purpose

This bathroom is very basic. There's a toilet and a sink. That's it. We know exactly what can be done in the quarter bath: use the toilet or use the sink. Comparing this to your business, you must know what your business does in a very basic way and be able to state it in one or two simple sentences. This simple statement is often referred to as a mission statement or purpose statement.

Mission statements that rank among the best are clear, memorable and concise. Top social profit organizations can explain what they do in fewer than 10 words. Most do not exceed 25. The shortest examples uses two words. Check out those that rank amongst the best:

Infrastructure: Social Profit Biz Basics

- TED: Spreading Ideas. (2 words)
- Smithsonian: The increase and diffusion of knowledge. (6 words)
- USO: lifts the spirits of America's troops and their families. (9 words)
- Livestrong: To inspire and empower people affected by cancer. (8)
- The Humane Society: Celebrating Animals, Confronting Cruelty. (4)
- Best Friends Animal Society: A better world through kindness to animals. (7)
- Public Broadcasting System (PBS): To create content that educates, informs and inspires. (8)
- American Heart Association: To build healthier lives, free of cardiovascular diseases and stroke. (10)
- Kiva: We are a non-profit organization with a mission to connect people through lending to alleviate poverty. (16)

Each of these mission / purpose statements informs the potential donor and your clients of exactly what the core social profit idea or principle is. When reading these statements of the organizations above, the missions are very clear without a lot of flowery substance. If you don't have a mission statement or if it's rather wordy and unclear, take some time to play with the ideas around what you do. See if you can create a strong and powerful statement in less than 10 words. Share the idea with your constituents to see if it resonates. Remember, when we don't clearly define what we do, customers and donors are left to wonder. When people wonder – they wander – and expect more or less than what's available.

BBB Tool 1: Know what you do and write it in a clearly defined mission statement.

How Do You Do It?
Half Bath – Policies & Procedures

The half bathroom is an extension of the quarter bath but usually includes a shower in addition to the toilet and the sink. This bathroom can also include cabinets for storage.

In the social profit world of business, the half bath is the extension of your mission / purpose statement. It not only explains what you do, but how you do it. Explaining how the business is run is a result of creating good policies and procedures. Often known as P&Ps,

these documented tools allow anyone reviewing your business to understand how you do what you do. This is important in several areas. When you have good Policies and Procedures, your team has a road map of how you want your business run. Policies and Procedures can be as simple and detailed as having a script that explains how to answer the phone. For example, here's an idea policy for greeting callers:

1. Pick up the phone before the 3rd ring.
2. Smile when you answer the phone.
3. Be as cheerful and helpful to customers/donors as possible. (Example: "Good TIME OF DAY, this is NAME, and you've reached ABC Company, how can you I help you?")
4. Assist the caller with direct information as often as possible.
5. Transfer the caller only if you cannot find the answer.
6. When transferring or ending the call in any way use the following script or something similar. (Example: "It was a pleasure servicing you and I hope you have a great day. Remember working with us is as easy as ABC!)
7. Wait for caller to respond or hang up before you hang up.

Customers enjoy receiving consistent service and Policies and Procedures assure that your business is handled in the same way at all times.

Using your Policies and Procedures can also confirm that you are doing business efficiently. Having documented how you do business can be a good defense when someone accuses you of doing something out of the nature of your business. This is also a wonderful training and evaluation tool for employees. When employees know exactly how they are to handle situations, they are more likely to perform in the correct way.

Of course, as in any bathroom, sometimes there may be a leaky faucet or a toilet that doesn't flush quite the way it's supposed to. In these instances, your P&Ps should equip staff with the means to handle out of the ordinary situations. Employees are empowered when they know there's an option in a situation that goes awry or is out of the ordinary. Just like in the bathroom, a plunger or a sign giving directions can avoid embarrassment.

BBB Tool 2: Write down how your business is run and how you expect your staff to behave in

conducting business. Create policies and procedures.

Where Are You Headed?
Full Bath – Goals / Objectives / Vision

In the full bath, everything is available – toilet, sink, shower and bath. There are storage cabinets and many times lots of extras like upgraded faucets and mirrors. In the social profit business structure, the full bath is how you see your business and what you want it to be. In short, the full bath is everything that was in the quarter and half baths plus future thinking. This future thinking is referred to as goals, objectives, visioning and strategic planning. Even though each serves a different purpose, the end result is the same – clear ideas on what you will do with your business and how you plan on doing it. These steps are important because they offer a road map to where your business is headed. And just like when you take a good book in the bathroom because you know you'll be there for a while, these steps will allow you to be more efficient in the business process with your time and energy.

Of course, with this all-inclusive bathroom, you will need to assure that it's in the right location, the equipment is operational to do what you need it to do, and you must be ready with a plan of action in keeping the bathroom in order. In the social profit business world, good Goals and Objectives are set as this plan of action and a destination or time frame is attached. These goals and objectives may change over time, but they are best when marked. To create the best goals and objectives, many companies use the S.M.A.R.T. methodology to define goals:

☐ Specific ideas of what you want to do. (Clean the toilet.)

☐ Measurable actions. (Clean with sponges & soap.)

☐ Achievable steps that can be met. (Purchase cleaning materials.)

☐ Realistic goals that are clear. (Clean once a week.)

☐ Timely goals that have deadlines. (Clean every Sat. at 8 a.m.)

You can see SMART goals are pretty clear and define what needs to be done, how to do it, and when it will be done in a snapshot. Try some SMART goals for some of the simple tasks that need to be done in your business. Something as simple as how you greet customers can be applied in a SMART goal and help with your bottom line as customers are greeted in a more consistent, pleasant way.

To grow your business further implement SMARTER or SMARTY goals. The "E" stands for Enthusiasm around your goal and a triple featured "R" allows Reward when goals are reached, Review of how they worked and Renewing the goals once achieved. The triple "R" in SMARTER goal setting enlivens your business goals regularly.

Another way of looking at SMART goals is to add a "Y" and make them SMARTY goals. In this instance, the "Y" stands for "Yours". When you and your team take ownership of their goals, then the magic starts to happen. Confirm these goals are what you want as a company or they will be neglected and never find completion.

BBS Tool 3: Write SMARTY and SMARTER goals for your team.

Chapter Two:
Investments & Payoffs

Bathroom: Keep Your Bathroom Current & Functional.

Business: Invest in your business.

When purchasing a house, many people like to remodel. One of the best investments in remodeling is to bring the bathroom into a current state. Investing in a bathroom remodel yields a 62 percent return, on average, but you've got to do it right according to an article in HomeAdvisor.com. Many homebuyers look for a master bathroom with two sinks, custom showers, and great lighting. Buyers are turned off with outdated bathrooms requiring a lot of work. Sometimes the remodel is as simple as a new paint job with a new toilet and fixtures. The main point is: an investment in a bathroom makes a big difference in the value of your house.

The same can be said for your business. Small investments in assuring the foundation is solid will be critical in running a successful business.

Foundation includes the basics learned in Chapter One of a solid Mission, Policies & Procedures, and Vision but it also includes the resources and tools that you need at your disposal to do the work that you do. Take for example if you need a plumber to clear a bathroom drain at your house. You expect this plumber to come with professional tools that will clear drains.

Besides screwdrivers, hammers and such, you expect that plumber to have a snake that will get your drain running clearly. Nowadays, plumbers even use scopes that can be placed in the drain to see what's actually backing them up. Now what if that plumber came to your house with a bottle of Drano and poured it down the pipe waiting for the drain to clear? Tell the truth – you would be ready to kick his behind out of your house!

The same is true in the social profit industry. Whatever service or product you provide, you should have the tools necessary so that your social profit runs efficiently. If you work with babies or children, then you need to have the appropriate number of people working with the children that your state ratio requires for the work you do. Basically, you need people who know how to work with children. If you work with rescue animals there are certain tools you'll need to take them in – cages, gloves, first aid kits, etc. Whatever your business, you need to know what tools and resources you need to run the business that you are in. The same goes for product based businesses. When Baskin Robbins says they have 31 flavors then there should be a plethora of flavors available when you go to purchase ice cream. Whatever you say you do in your business, be prepared to do it well. If that means you must invest in the tools to do that, then you must invest.

Investments can be in people, time, equipment, and even education. In today's digital age, computer systems and phone services are some of the most important tools any business can have. Nothing angers a customer more than not being able to get through in a timely and efficient manner. Use professionals when investing in your business. That doesn't mean a small business can't get the job done, just assure they have the tools needed to service you.

Infrastructure: Social Profit Biz Basics

The top three Basic Business tools & resources essential for most social profits are:

- Strategic Plan
- Finance / Accounting
- Operations / Technology & Facilities

Most new social profits do not acquire the proper tools and resources to run their business because they believe they lack the funds. As they continue to grow, the need to invest becomes an even further stretch because they become used to doing without them. This inefficiency doesn't make the business better – it makes it harder. Many times it stresses the leadership when the business is not properly invested in.

The basic tools to invest in for any social profit can make a world of difference in how the organization grows. Creating these tools requires a clear understanding of your business and, when used properly, will give you a good foundation for your social profit.

Strategic Plan

Now, what could I possibly learn in the bathroom that involves Strategic Planning? It's not always the similarities of the bathroom that teach you lessons, but also the differences. Let me explain. When you go in the bathroom, you definitely go in with a plan in mind of what you're going to do. However, the plan for the bathroom – for the most part – is very isolated. You can get a lot done there and it's absolutely meaningful work that should be done alone, but you don't want to blast what goes on there from the rafters.

In the social profit world, you want everyone to know what you do and how to support it. So it's exactly the opposite from the bathroom planning experience – and therein lies the lesson. The bathroom planning investment is an isolated one and the social profit business experience is an all-inclusive one. Both are important investments of time and energy and both will result in a healthier state.

The strategic plan is just as important as the Mission, Vision and Policies & Procedures and in fact is the way to get those areas in action and accomplished. That's all the Strategic Plan is—a way to get the job done. There is no right or wrong way to get this document done but a collaborative process with the board of directors, staff and leadership is suggested, so that everyone has buy-in to the goals that will be set in the plan. The Strategic Planning process is just as important as the plan. It should not be created by one person in a vacuum and, the more input to the plan, the more likely the organization will achieve what the plan sets out to do.

The most important thing to remember about Strategic Planning is to stay in alignment with your mission and vision throughout the plan. Keep your mission seated in the room with you. Use business tools like a SWOT Analysis (Strengths, Weaknesses, Opportunities, Threats) to determine the organizations current state. You can also do an overall Organizational Assessment. The plan should include your goals, strategies and tactics for the next 3-5 years along with an income and expense budget. Most important as the plan is complete, include an implementation or roll out strategy.

BBB Tool 4: Work with your Board to create a solid vision and SMART Strategic Plan mapping where your business is headed.

Finance / Accounting

Good and sound financial management is basically good plumbing in the bathroom. The key to everything going down the drain is to check that the pipes work effectively. The key to success for any social profit organization is to check that the money is working effectively. This includes having clear accounting practices that allow you to determine the health of your business. Put internal controls in place to ensure that your financial books are in order, accurate, and credible. This is an area where you should hire someone if you are not comfortable with bookkeeping and financial management.

Start with a budget for the organization. Many people are afraid of the word budget but, in all honesty, a budget is nothing more than a spending plan. It tells you how you plan to spend money that you have. It also shows you when you don't have the money to spend. Budgets tell you what assets and cash on hand are available and the expenses that need to be charged against those funds. The budget is compared to your actual financials and, with these numbers side-by- side, you can learn a lot about your business by using some relatively simple ratios.

The quick ratio gives an indicator of your organizations ability to meet short-term obligations. A quick ratio of 1 or more is good. The debt ratio tells the proportion of debt relative to assets. A debt ratio of 1 or less is good. The defensive interval ratio measures the number of days an organization can operate without having to tap into long-term (fixed) assets. Most experts recommend maintaining enough cash on hand to cover three to six months of operating expenses.

As you put your finances together, there are other areas in the finance and accounting area to stay on top of like the filing of your taxes. In the social profit world, taxes are filed through forms 990 or 990-EZ depending on your organizations financial status. These should be filed timely according to your fiscal year end.

Payroll is another area that is covered under Finance/Accounting and not only does this include paying staff members on time and properly, but submitting the proper payroll taxes too. Interest and penalties on payroll taxes add up quickly so verify that this is done in an efficient manner.

BBB Tool 5: Ask for sample budgets from other social profits similar to yours to see what categories they expense and work you're your Accountant to capture everything necessary.

Operations / Technology & Facilities

Finally, do you have everything you need to use your bathroom like you want? Does the toilet flush? Does the shower flow? Does the trash can close appropriately? Making sure your organization is operating under the standards that you've set is important. The facility that you operate in should be clean and secure. Insurances should be in place (liability, worker's comp, etc.) and permits current. Don't let technology drive you. It changes too frequently. Decide what you want to achieve and weigh the costs and benefits of incorporating new equipment. Your website is your face so keep it clean and easy to navigate while open enough to include email marketing, search engine optimization (SEO) and social media for the future. Don't rush into it all at one time – you will get lost.

Infrastructure: Social Profit Biz Basics

I just saw a newfangled sink in Home Depot last week and was tempted to call a contractor to have it installed because it was so pretty! Then I remembered, I just had my bathroom remodeled a year ago and it was functioning exactly like I wanted. There was nothing outdated or wrong with my sink so I didn't need a new one. Be careful jumping into every new trend. Throughout your operations, seek competitive pricing and quality service. Once you find vendors that work well with you, keep them on board and include them in your offerings. See if they are open to volunteering and being a part of the team. However, do not expect your vendors to offer their services for free. They are in business and, in order to help you stay in business, need to make their revenue as well. Every vendor might be a potential donor of something but allow them to do their business without having to give it away. This way, you can hold them accountable to the work they do without feeling like they did you a favor.

Chapter Three:
Create Fresh Approaches

Bathroom: Open the doors & windows to keep it fresh.

Business: Be open to new ideas and models to run your business.

As a bathroom analogy, I'd say this is how it comes and how it goes. Yep, this is where the nitty-gritty business of the bathroom happens. Now there are so many references that can be made that would provide humor and insight in this scenario, but I'm going to refrain from using most of them. Instead, let's just stick with "how it comes" and "how it goes" and agree that as we build our social profit infrastructure, ideas and stuff are going to come and go. Some of it is good and can be incorporated. Some of it is…. Well, some of it can be flushed.

Once you've completed your strategic plan you should feel a great sense of accomplishment because you have a document or a map to operate with. This map is a guide to running your business and helps you in so many other areas. You are at the beginning of building out a strong social profit that will last the test of time. Just because you've decided this is the way you're going to meet your goals doesn't mean it's clad in stone. This is a living document.

Living documents are open to change and refinement. If something isn't working, change it. The key to effective and meaningful change is communication.

Let's say that functional sink that I have in my bathroom is okay, but I still want a new one to make my bathroom experience more enjoyable. Well, I can add in my household plan a remodel with a new sink. I may need to get a buy-in from family members affected by it. Even if they're not paying for it, they can be inconvenienced if the sink is out of commission. Letting all parties know the plan of change is important. It helps to continue the buy-in and keep the plan on the table. The other thing it does is opens others to thinking about what the possibilities are.

While Executive Director at A Place Called Home in South Los Angeles, I found myself frustrated with those who pointed at the children in the community and called them "at-risk" -- as if they were not part of the overall Los Angeles landscape. I understood why this label was there, but believed it was misplaced because these children were much more than the at-risk community that they lived in. Labels have impact so, in a newsletter to our supporters I wrote an article titled, "I'm Possible verses Impossible Odds." The piece concluded that the children we served were "at-promise" verses "at-risk" and they were resilient enough to survive an at-risk, community, which made them "I'm Possible Heroes." The response was tremendous and we raised more money on that appeal than ever before. It was a new way of thinking about our old mission. I challenged people to see our kids differently and I challenge you to see your business differently.

I was told once "It's not what they call you – it's what you answer to." Though I get that statement in terms of knowing who you are, I think it's also important for people to understand what they should call you. Having a difficult name, I'm always challenged with correcting people from saying it wrong. But if I don't correct them... if I don't inform them... if I don't challenge them to see my name differently – then they never will.

Infrastructure: Social Profit Biz Basics

It can be said with your social profit that if you keep the status quo and never look at different options then no one will ever see the possibilities you might offer. Open your mind to new ideas even when you've laid out the best plans ever. Listen to newcomers and those that have been with you for the long term. There is always something fresh on the horizon. Be ready to grow.

Be ready to grow in different directions, at different times, and with a variety of people.

Always remember to keep it real. In the bathroom, we let it rip, right? It's our private space where we can be ourselves–without shame or embarrassment–it's our space! And when we're done (with a shower or from a toilet break) we feel fresher. By the time we're totally done, we open the doors and the windows to bring in natural air, light and refreshment. It's authentic and real. Keep it real in your business too. Open the doors and windows and keep it fresh! When you are doing what you were born to do, there is nothing to be ashamed of. Your business should be an open book. Hey, as a social profit your financials are all over the web anyway when you file your 990s.

Be a proud social profit! When the revenues are not what you would like them to be, communicate with your accountant to add a statement as to why with your 990's. There's nothing wrong with having low revenue – the problem is not keeping good records. Be accountable. In short, be authentic. Nothing speaks to donors and supporters more than the authenticity of leaders of social profits. When being authentic, I find social profit leaders to be inspiring and effective at getting support for the work they do.

BBB Tool 6: Be authentic and do what you say you do. Ask for help when you need it.

Summary

Hopefully, you enjoyed this read but mostly I hope you learned good tools for a solid foundation and infrastructure of your business. In the social profit world, there are many ways to build your business but having a steady foundation is crucial. Sequel books straight from the bathroom will include communications, fundraising, human resources, boards and programs.

Many people told me they thought only of the toilet when they read the title of this book. I thought that was funny and also a great lesson – never underestimate the power of the bathroom as a three dimensional space!

Think about how many people look at your business as a one-dimensional model when you have so many working parts going on. Well, this book was designed to broaden your perspective-- especially if you were one of those who picked it up for toilet jokes.

From reading this book, I hope you learned the 3 essential elements to building the infrastructure of your business:

Infrastructure: Social Profit Biz Basics

- ☐ Know where you are & what you do.
- ☐ Invest in your business.
- ☐ Be open to new ideas and models to run your business.

Following the guides from these areas will assure that your Mission and Vision statements are in place as well as Policies and Procedures. They will also reflect that your business operates with the most important resources of finance and a strategic plan. Finally, being open to new ideas and models to run your business will help you see future areas of growth.

See www.beyond-story.com for more social profit information.